# First Fabulous Facts

# Space

Written by Anita Ganeri
Illustrated by Patrizia Donaera
Cartoon illustrations by Jane Porter

Consultant: Colin Stuart, astronomer and science writer

A catalogue record for this book is available from the British Library

Published by Ladybird Books Ltd
80 Strand, London, WC2R 0RL
A Penguin Company

001
© LADYBIRD BOOKS LTD MMXIV
LADYBIRD and the device of a Ladybird are trademarks of Ladybird Books Ltd

ISBN: 978-0-72328-853-4

Printed in China

 # Contents

# The solar system

We live on Planet Earth – a huge lump of rock in space. But Earth is not on its own. It is part of a solar system of eight planets that orbit (go round) the Sun.

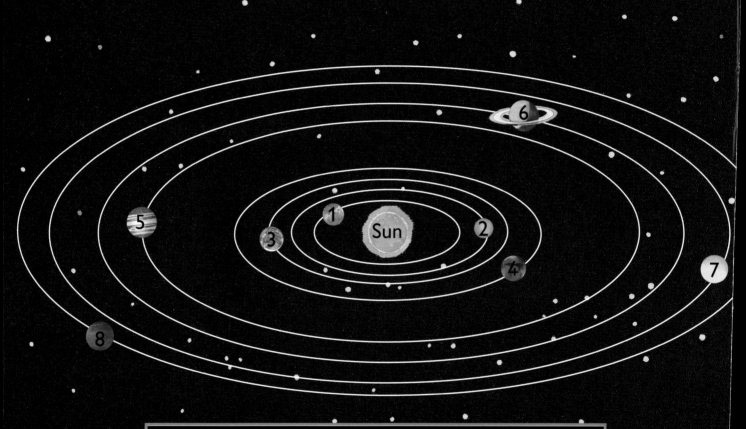

Key: 1 = Mercury  2 = Venus   3 = Earth    4 = Mars
     5 = Jupiter  6 = Saturn  7 = Uranus  8 = Neptune

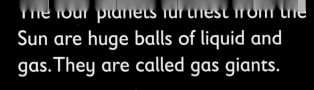

The four planets closest to the Sun are made from earth and rock. They are called rocky planets.

The four planets furthest from the Sun are huge balls of liquid and gas. They are called gas giants.

ercury      Venus      Earth      Mars          Jupiter      Saturn      Uranus      Neptune

## Milky space

Our solar system is part of an enormous group of stars called the Milky Way galaxy. You can see the cloudy, white band of the Milky Way on a clear night.

## Wow!

The solar system is very old indeed. Most scientists think it was made about 4,600 billion years ago, when a giant cloud of gas and dust crashed together.

BANG!

# Sun and stars

The Sun is a star – a giant ball of glowing gas that gives off huge amounts of heat and light. When you look at the sky at night, the tiny specks of light you see are also stars, like the Sun, but very far away.

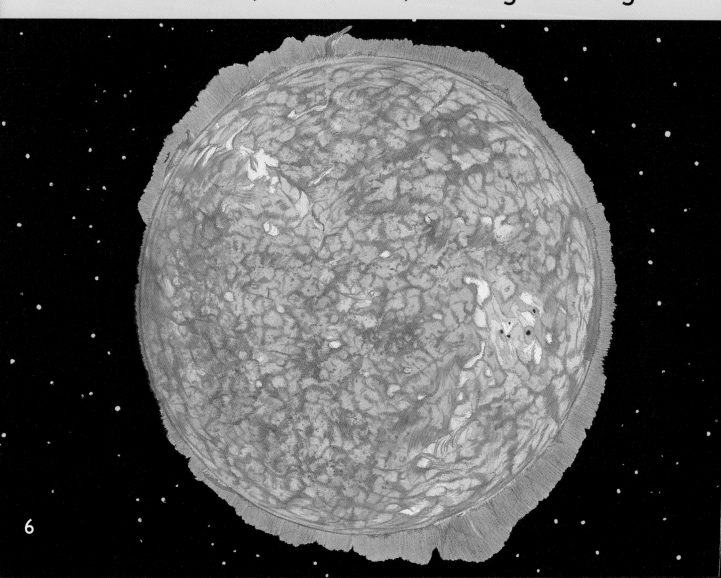

# Fabulous Facts

## Sky shapes

The stars in the night sky appear to make patterns, that we call constellations. The ancient Greeks named them after animals, objects or people that they looked like.

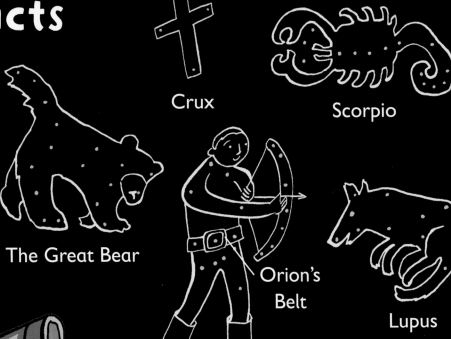

Crux

Scorpio

The Great Bear

Orion's Belt

Lupus

Orion

My turn, please!

Wow, that's cool!

## Star scope

A telescope can make objects in space look up to twenty-five times closer to you.

## Wow!

The Sun won't keep shining forever. In about 5 billion years (a very, very long time), scientists think it will start to get bigger and swallow up the planets.

GULP!

7

# Mercury

Mercury is the smallest planet. It has a rocky surface covered in craters. This is caused by asteroids and comets crashing into it.

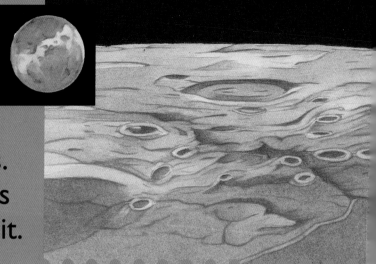

# Fabulous Facts

## Mercury stats

**Size:**
4,879 kilometres across
(three times smaller than Earth)

**Distance from the Sun:**
58 million kilometres
(three times closer than Earth)

**Length of a year:**
eighty-eight Earth days

**Named after:**
the Roman god of messages

## Wow!

Mercury is the planet that is closest to the Sun. The side that faces the Sun is baking hot. The other side is freezing cold.

Phew!

Brrrrr!

# Venus

Venus has some of the worst weather in our solar system! It is roasting hot and smothered in thick, yellow clouds full of acid.

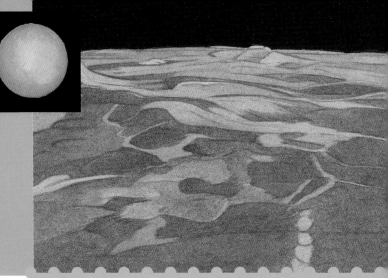

## Fabulous Facts

### Venus stats

**Size:**
12,100 kilometres across
(almost the same size as Earth)

**Distance from the Sun:**
108 million kilometres
(one and a half times closer than Earth)

**Length of a year:**
225 Earth days

**Named after:**
the Roman goddess
of love and beauty

### Wow!

Venus is known as the Morning or Evening Star. This is because the light from the Sun makes it looks like a bright star at sunrise or just after sunset.

Goodnight, Evening Star!

9

# Earth

As far as we know, Earth is the only place in our solar system where there is life. People, plants and animals are able to live on Earth because it has air and water, and is warmed by the Sun.

towns and cities

countryside

seas and oceans

forests and jungles

# Fabulous Facts

Sun

Earth

Moon

## Keep on spinning

Earth spins round on its axis once every twenty-four hours. When your part of the world is facing the Sun, it is day-time. When it is facing away from the Sun, you have night-time.

## A watery world

Earth is a lot more watery than its name suggests. About three times more of the surface is covered in water than land!

That's a lot of water!

## Earth stats

**Size:**
12,756 kilometres across
**Distance from the Sun:**
150 million kilometres
**Length of a year:**
365 days
**Named after:** a word that means 'the ground'

## Wow!

Scientists call Earth a 'Goldilocks' planet. This is because it is just the right distance from the Sun. It is not too hot and not too cold for life to survive here.

That's our planet!

It's just right!

11

# Earth's Moon

The Moon is the nearest object to our planet in space. As it orbits Earth, it spins once on its own axis, which means we only ever see one side of the Moon. It is a dry, dusty place with no air to breathe.

Moon crater

# Fabulous Facts

## Moon month

As the Moon orbits, the side of it that faces Earth is sometimes lit up by sunshine. Other times it is not. This makes the Moon appear to change shape through the month. These are called the Moon's phases.

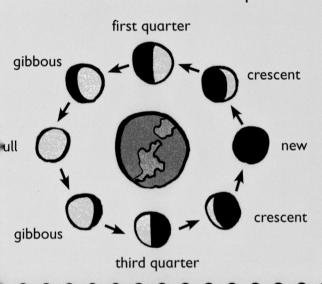

first quarter
gibbous
crescent
full
new
gibbous
crescent
third quarter

## Solar shadow

A solar eclipse happens when the Moon passes right between the Sun and Earth, and makes a shadow.

## Moon stats

**Size:** 3,476 kilometres across (three and a half times smaller than Earth)
**Distance from Earth:** 384,000 kilometres
**Length of a year:** twenty-seven Earth days
**Named after:** an old word that means 'month'

Calendar
1 2 3 4 5 6 7
8 9 10 11 12 13 14
15 16 17 18 19 20 21
22 23 24 25 26 27

## Wow!

Astronauts first walked on the Moon in 1969. The footprints they left are still there because there is no wind or rain to blow or wash them away!

Wait for me!

# Mars

Mars, like Earth, has clouds and winds. There are deserts, too. Life might have existed on Mars long, long ago, but scientists have not found anything living there today.

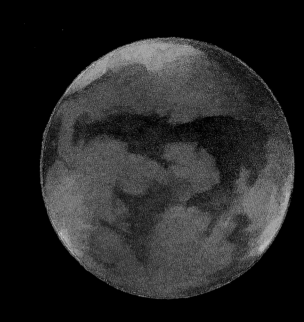

## Grandest canyon

There is a giant canyon on Mars' surface called Valles Marineris. Canyons are usually made by water, so scientists think there was once water on Mars.

## The red planet

Mars is known as the red planet. The red colour is caused by rusty metal found in dust and rocks on the planet's surface.

Valles Marineris

# Fabulous Facts

## Mars stats

**Size:** 6,794 kilometres across
(half the size of Earth)
**Distance from the Sun:**
228 million kilometres
(twice as far as Earth)
**Length of a year:**
two Earth years
**Named after:**
the Roman god of war

## Mars machine

Scientists have sent spacecraft to explore Mars. The Curiosity rover is a remote-controlled vehicle sent to study the planet's surface.

Left a bit, right a bit!

## Wow!

Olympus Mons is a volcano on Mars. At about 25 kilometres high, it is three times taller than Earth's tallest mountain, Mount Everest!

## Space spuds

Mars has two small moons called Phobos and Deimos. They look like giant potatoes!

Phobos

Deimos

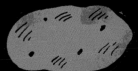

# Jupiter

Jupiter is the biggest planet in the solar system. It is a giant ball of liquid and gas, with a very violent, stormy atmosphere.

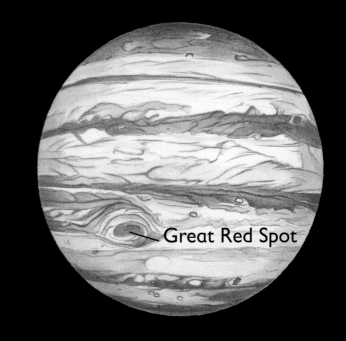

Great Red Spot

## Fabulous Facts

### Jupiter stats

**Size**: 143 thousand kilometres across (eleven times bigger than Earth)

**Distance from the Sun:** 779 million kilometres (five times further than Earth)

**Length of a year:** twelve Earth years

**Named after:** the Roman king of the gods

### Red storm

The Great Red Spot is an enormous storm, three times bigger than Earth.

### Wow!

At the last count, Jupiter had sixty-seven moons but scientists may still discover more

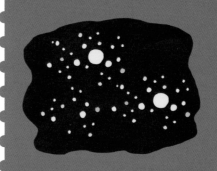

66, 67, 68?

# Saturn

Saturn is the second largest planet in the solar system. It has six main rings and thousands of smaller ones round it.

## Fabulous Facts

### Saturn stats

**Size:** 121 thousand kilometres across (nine times bigger than Earth)

**Distance from the Sun:** 1,434 million kilometres (nine times further than Earth)

**Length of a year:** thirty Earth years

**Named after:** the Roman god of farming

### Ice rings

Saturn's rings are made of billions of small pieces of ice.

### Wow!

Saturn is a giant planet but it is so light that it would float in water. But only if you could find a bucket large enough!

Is it my turn?

No, it's Sa-turn!

# Uranus and Neptune

Uranus and Neptune are the last two planets in the solar system. Both these planets are so far away from the Sun that they are always freezing cold.

## Uranus

Because of the way that Uranus spins on its axis, nights on some parts of the planet can last for up to forty years!

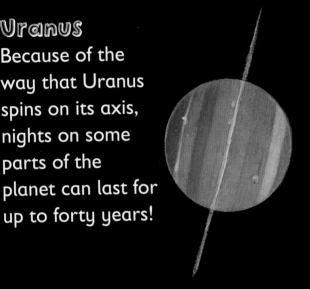

## Uranus stats

**Size:** 51,000 kilometres (four times bigger than Earth)
**Distance from the Sun:** 2,873 million kilometres (nineteen times further than Earth)
**Length of a year:** eighty-four Earth years
**Named after:** the ancient Greek god of the sky

## Neptune

The winds on Neptune can blow as fast as 2,000 kilometres per hour. They are the fastest winds in the solar system.

## Neptune stats

**Size:** 49,000 kilometres (almost four times bigger than Earth)
**Distance from the Sun:** 4,495 million kilometres (thirty times further than Earth)
**Length of a year:** 185 Earth years
**Named after:** the Roman god of the se

# Beyond Neptune

The solar system does not stop when you get to Neptune. Beyond Neptune, there are hundreds of smaller objects that orbit the Sun – dwarf planets.

## Poor Pluto

A planet has its own orbit. A dwarf planet shares its orbit with other objects. In 2006, scientists decided that Pluto is a dwarf planet.

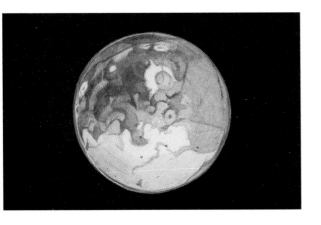

## Belt up!

Pluto lies at the outer edge of the solar system, in a huge area of frozen space rocks called the Kuiper Belt.

## Wow!

New Horizons is a space probe on a mission to study Pluto and its five moons. It set out from Earth in 2006.

Pluto, where are you?

# Space rocks

The planets and moons are not the only things in orbit in the solar system. There are also millions of other objects out there. Asteroids are big lumps of rock and metal. Comets are like giant, dusty snowballs.

comets

asteroids

# Fabulous Facts

## Ring of rocks

Between Mars and Jupiter, there are millions of asteroids in a ring. This ring is called the asteroid belt.

Jupiter

Mars

## Star show

Meteors are bits of rock that hurtle from space to Earth. Most meteors burn up in the atmosphere, making a streak of light called a shooting star.

Make a wish!

## Halley's Comet

Halley's Comet is visible from Earth about every seventy-five years. Astronomer Edmond Halley discovered this in 1705.

## Wow!

A crater more than 1 kilometre across can be seen in Arizona, USA. It was made by a meteorite smashing into Earth about 50,000 years ago.

Wow!

21

# Exploring Space

The solar system is huge. It takes months or years to reach the other planets. Space probes have visited many planets and moons, but so far the only place astronauts have landed is on Earth's Moon.

astronaut

lunar lander

# Fabulous Facts

## Goodbye, Earth

The first person to go into space was Yuri Gagarin, from Russia. In 1961, he flew round Earth for an hour in his Vostok spacecraft.

## Super shuttles

Between 1981 and 2011, 135 space flights were made by space shuttles. Space shuttles can travel to space and return many times.

## Wow!

In September 1968, Zond 5 became the first spacecraft to fly round the Moon and return to Earth. On board were two tortoises, some flies, some worms and some plants. They all returned alive!

# Living in space

Astronauts and scientists live on the International Space Station high above Earth. Eating, drinking, sleeping and washing are all difficult in space. People and objects just float about!

# Fabulous Facts

## Sticky snacks

Astronauts have to eat food that sticks together, such as stew and scrambled eggs. Dry food breaks up into crumbs that float off!

## Wrap up well

Astronauts sometimes have to go outside the Space Station to make repairs. There is no air in space, so they wear spacesuits to help them breathe. Spacesuits also protect them from the heat of the Sun.

## Wow!

In space, your skeleton does not have to support your weight. This means that your bones can stretch out and you become a few centimetres taller.

# Is there anybody out there?

There is a lot more to discover beyond our solar system. Scientists use radio telescopes to search for signals from outer space. Other telescopes in space look for different worlds and, possibly, even aliens!

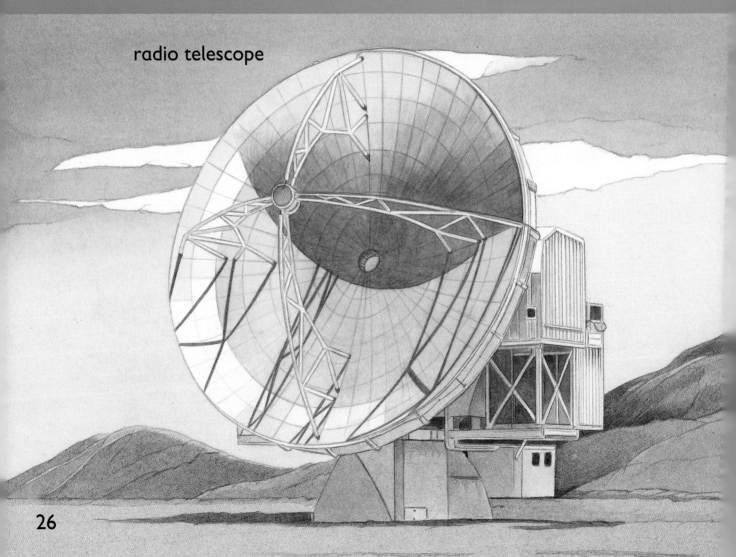

radio telescope

# Fabulous Facts

## Another Earth?

There are many billions of planets in our galaxy. Scientists think some of them could be just like Earth!

## Looking for life

SETI (Search for Extraterrestrial Intelligence) is a scientific project that looks for alien life. If an alien was found, what do you think it would look like?

BLARP!

U! F! O!

## Flying fact or fiction?

UFO means 'Unidentified Flying Object'. Some people think that UFOs come from other planets, but this has not been proved.

## Wow!

The Voyager space probes are travelling through the solar system and beyond. On board are messages from Earth, which might be discovered by aliens, millions of years in the future.

27

# Record breakers

## Free floater

In 1984, Bruce McCandless used a
special backpack to fly around in space.
He was the first astronaut to go outside
a spacecraft and not be attached to it.

## Moon drive

In July 1971, Apollo 15 astronauts David Scott and James Irwin took
a lunar rover to the Moon. They were the first people to drive
somewhere other than on Earth!

## Super Sirius

Sirius is the brightest star in the sky. It is in the Great Dog constellation and is known as the 'Dog Star'.

Sirius

## First female astronaut

The first woman in space was Valentina Tereshkova from Russia. She was on the Vostok 6 mission that launched on 16 June 1963 and orbited Earth forty-eight times.

## Bon voyager!

On 25 August 2012, the space probe Voyager 1 left the solar system. It was the first man-made object to do so.

# Galactic gags!

**When has the Moon had enough to eat?**

When it is full!

**What songs do the planets sing?**

Nep-tunes!

**What did Jupiter say to Saturn?**

Give me a ring sometime!

**When do astronauts eat lunch?**

At launch time!

**Where did the astronaut park his spaceship?**

At the parking meteor!

**How does the solar system hold up its trousers?**

With an asteroid belt!

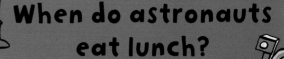

# Glossary

**astronaut**  A person specially trained to travel and work in space.

**astronomer**  A person who studies space.

**atmosphere**  The gases that surround a planet.

**axis**  An imaginary line that runs through a planet or moon, on which it spins.

**constellation**  A group of stars in the sky that is thought to look like, and is named after, an object, person or animal.

**crater**  A hollow area on a planet or moon, usually created by something crashing into the surface.

**galaxy**  A collection of billions of stars and other objects.

**meteorite**  A piece of rock, usually from an asteroid or comet, that survives after crashing into Earth.

**orbit**  The path of one object as it travels round another.

**probe**  An unmanned spacecraft, sent into space to do research.

**solar system**  All the planets, moons and other objects that go round the Sun. Earth is part of the solar system.

# Index